To Peter
Thank you !

M000192094

LIVING THE LORD'S
PRAYER

Be Blessed !

Creating the Powerful Habit of Prayer in Your Life

Michael Heath

sermonto**book**
.com

Sermon To Book
www.sermontobook.com

Living the Lord's Prayer / Michael Heath
ISBN-13: 978-0692552544
ISBN-10: 0692552545

To my Lord and Savior Jesus Christ for saving me, filling me, calling me and gifting me; you allow me to see a miracle every time I preach your word.

To my wife, Crystal, your love, support and belief in me pushes me to be greater and to want more. You are my "Good Thing" and my best friend. Thank you!

To my children: Sharia, Michael, Ciara and Joshua. Thank you for always believing in my dreams!

To Living Waters Ministries, you were birthed out of my love for God's people. Thank you for allowing me to lead you as God leads me. Thank you for giving me the weekly opportunity to share God's word with you.

To those who have contributed to this project through prayer and encouragement, I am eternally grateful. Especially Charmelia Bond, Loida Hopkins, Alicia McDaniel and Jacqueline Seaton; your edits have aided in bringing this book to fruition.

To Dr. Malcolm Walls, your friendship and encouragement were invaluable in the production of this work.

CONTENTS

Introduction

Growing up I was taught that I should pray but I was never really taught how to pray. As a result, I was a very nominal Christian concerning my prayer life even after I got saved. Of course, I believed that God was all powerful but I never acted as such. This belief, while real, never really impacted my day to day life. I would pray with little to no expectation that God would move in my situations. That is until my oldest son Michael had a terrible seizure. One evening while I was driving, he stopped breathing and his eyes rolled back into his head. His little body shook, he was three years old at the time, and I have never felt such fear in my life. At that moment, I learned the power of genuine prayer. My prayer wasn't based on religious verbiage but on my faith and relationship with God. I prayed, "God touch my son." God honored my prayer and my son started breathing again at that instant.

Ever since that incident, which took place in 1994, I have taken my prayer life seriously. Prayer has been central to my walk with Christ and I credit many of the blessings I enjoy to answered prayer. Prayer has become so natural that I often ask people if I can pray for them.

One day I committed to praying with everyone I spoke with on the phone. I prayed with family, friends, a telemarketer and even a person who called the wrong number. I was blessed and so were those I prayed with.

I have taught and preached on prayer many times. It is my desire to reignite the fire of prayer within the body of Christ. This book began as a sermon series which I preached over a five-week period at the church I pastor called Living Waters. I went through the Lord's Prayer verse by verse. The response was amazing and many in the congregation were blessed and challenged; resulting in phenomenal growth in their prayer lives. I believe that prayer is the most powerful yet most underutilized weapon we have as Christians. Jesus, who was God in the flesh, prayed several times every day. How do we as Christians feel we can cope with the struggles in life if we don't spend time in prayer?

This book is written with both the serious Bible student and the new convert in mind. It is not meant to be an academic book but a practical book that will challenge the reader to move toward a deeper prayer life. By examining the specific aspects of the Lord's Prayer, the reader will gain a better understanding of what is expected when praying.

The questions at the end of each chapter are designed to engage the reader in reflection and discussion, and the summary that follows each set of questions is geared toward practical application of the principles in this book. Being a disciple is a lifelong endeavor.

— *Pastor Michael Heath, 2015*

The Secret of Prayer

Then the Lord God said, 'It is not good for the man to be alone; I will make him a helper suitable for him.' — **Genesis 2:18**

In our contemporary Christian culture, prayer is often ignored or at least relegated to a background action. We may bookend our day with short prayers, however the busyness of life often crowds prayer out of our daily routine. This is not only relegated to the individual but even many churches tend to focus more on the worship service than on prayer. Do not get me wrong, worship is necessary. Singing is good; celebrating is good; praising God is good; shouting is good—but prayer is better. When we are physically or mentally unable to worship in the manner we are most comfortable, we should still be able to pray.

As humans, we are relational beings. Genesis 2:18 says, "Then the Lord God said, "It is not good for the man to be alone; I will make him a helper suitable for him." Not only did He design for us to be involved in interpersonal relationships with one another, He also created us to be in a relationship with Him.

It is my prayer that as you read this book you see that your connection with God is a spiritual one and not one that is based on a physical connection in the natural realm. That is why prayer is so essential to your daily Christian walk. It is the way Christians develop a healthy relationship with Him.

Lord, teach us to pray

Prayer is not just communication, worship, and submission. It is more than that. It is our link to God.

Matthew 6:7-15 states, "And when you are praying, do not use meaningless repetition as the Gentiles do, for they suppose that they will be heard for their many words. So do not be like them; for your Father knows what you need before you ask Him. Pray, then, in this way:

"Our Father who is in heaven,

Hallowed be Your name.

Your kingdom come.

Your will be done,

On earth as it is in heaven.

Give us this day our daily bread.

And forgive us our debts, as we also have forgiven our debtors.

And do not lead us into temptation, but deliver us from evil. For Yours is the kingdom and the power and the glory forever. Amen."

Notice Jesus never says, "If you pray." He says, "*when* you pray." If we made a timeline of Jesus's life, we would see that He prayed to His Father more than He did anything else—more than teaching, healing, or feeding people. Jesus understood the power of being connected to the Father in prayer.

What about us? How often do we stop and acknowledge God during our day? Five minutes a day? Maybe less? Prayer should be an integral part of our everyday life because like Jesus, our power comes from being connected to the Father. Our connectivity increases our productivity.

As quoted earlier, Jesus instructs us not to pray with meaningless repetition. Many of us have had the experience of trying to read something while our mind was elsewhere. After a while, we thought, "I have read this page three times and I don't even know what I just read." That is what it is like to pray without thinking. Jesus does not want our "autopilot prayers." He wants us to speak sincerely from our hearts. Praying sincerely opens our heart to God and allows Him to open His heart to us, which sets the tone for our prayer life.

Prayer Cannot Be Routine

Have any of the following become habits in your life?

- Squeezing in a quick prayer before bed.

- Saying a quick prayer on your way to work.

- Saying grace hurriedly before a meal,

We often pray out of habit. When prayer becomes routine, it can lose its meaning. We have to push through the busyness of life—the phone calls, the meetings, the TV shows, the bills—and focus on the Lord. When we pray, it is best to eliminate as many distractions as we can. True fellowship with the Lord comes in the intimacy of prayer, but we cannot achieve that intimacy in an environment filled with commotion or other distractions such as the TV being on, people talking, or our children making noise. These distractions will inevitably leave us offering God only a hurried superficial prayer over a meal or a quick prayer at bedtime.

In Luke 11, the disciples asked Jesus to teach them how to pray because they noticed that He prayed differently than them. His prayers were relational, rather than ritualistic.

Being real with God allows Him to meet us at our point of struggle and calm all of our fears and anxieties.

The disciples did not ask to be taught how to pray because they did not know how to pray, instead they wanted to pray like Jesus. The disciples were Jewish men who grew up under Mosaic Levitical Judaism. They learned all the proper prayers, feast days and Jewish sacrifices. From Jesus however, they learned that God does not want us to recite empty words. He wants us to pour ourselves out to Him with passion and desire, not out of a ritualistic duty.

Many of us are familiar with the prayer we learned as children: Now I lay me down to sleep, I pray the Lord my soul to keep, and if I die before I wake, I pray the Lord my soul to take.

This prayer is a good prayer for children learning to pray because it is easy to remember and is easily added to their bedtime routine. However, this is not an authentic prayer for the growing Christian. There is an expectation that we will "graduate" to praying prayers with more substance. God wants us to share our *hearts* with Him—our confusion, our questions, our worries, our joys, our failures—everything.

Be real with God. Tell Him everything. Life is not ritualistic. With every unique situation we will feel different emotions and face different fears. Being real with God allows Him to meet us at our point of struggle and calm all of our fears and anxieties.

The book of Psalms offers us a few examples of real prayers. One example is found in Psalm 55:6. Here the author cries out in despair and says, "If only I had wings like a dove! I would fly away and find rest." He is praying that God would allow him to be free from the persecution of his enemies. Yet by the time he closes his prayer he states, "But I call to God, and the LORD will save me." There is great power in prayer when our feelings are verbalized.

Open Your Mouth

There is something about speaking audibly to God. Over 127 times in scripture, we are told to praise God, and many times the meaning of the word "praise"— whether in Hebrew, Aramaic, or Greek—involves something verbal.

Hymn writer Charles Wesley said, "If I had ten thousand tongues, I couldn't praise You enough, not if I had ten thousand hands I couldn't praise You enough." Charles Wesley is saying that God deserves more praise than we could ever give Him.

God wants our praise and our prayers verbalized. He knows everything that is in our heart, but He desires us to put our feelings into words.

Think about it this way: My wife knows I love her, but what if I never told her? Would she like that? No! She wants to hear me say it out loud—and often. That's what God wants too! He enjoys hearing audible praise and prayers because it demonstrates to Him that we love and depend on Him. As Hebrews 13:15 states: "Therefore, through Him let us continually offer up to God a sacrifice of praise, that is, the fruit of our lips that confess His name."

Our Heavenly Daddy?

*Pray, then, in this way: 'Our Father who is in heaven, Hallowed be Your name.' — **Matthew 6:9***

When Jesus gave His disciples instruction on prayer, He made it very clear that prayer is personal. The first thing Jesus demonstrates is the closeness of His relationship with the Father in light of who God is.

First He said, "Our Father." The Greek word "Abba," is a word reserved for children, something like our English word "Daddy." That is pretty personal. That is a different kind of relationship: one that denotes closeness. The Jews referred to God as the self-existent one and the God of Abraham, Isaac, and Jacob. While these titles can make it appear as if God is faraway and untouchable, Jesus lets us know we can approach God on an intimate level. But do we come to Him on that intimate level? Do we say "You are my Savior, You are my God, and You are my redeemer?" Do we go even further and say, "Daddy, I need you?" That is the personal, familial relationship piece we so often shy away from. This type of focus from us provides the opportunity for God to respond just as intimately. The call of a child causes a parent to respond. My own experiences with my children have taught me the power of their call. One evening, I was at an event, and my daughter called me on my cell phone. I could hear in her voice how upset she was when she said, "Daddy!"

I said, "Hold on one second," and I immediately exited the event to find out what was wrong, and what I needed to do to help.

As a mortal man, I can only be in one place at one time, but the omnipresent, all-powerful God can be everywhere at once—including right by your side when you're hurting.

Why? Because my child was in trouble and called me. Loving parents always respond to their children. This is why loving mothers can discern the cry of their child in a room full of crying babies. God responds to our cries in the same way.

God knows our cry because we are family. Our relationship with God gives us an intimate bond that we cannot get elsewhere. And the wonderful thing is, that unlike a mortal man, who can only be in one place at a time, the omnipresent, all-powerful God can be everywhere at once—including right by our side when we are hurting. My child had to wait for my assistance because of my physical limitations, yet God can be there in an instant. This is an excellent reason why turning to God in every situation should be our first and automatic action. Unfortunately, we often try to conceal our problems from God because we think we can handle them on our own. Only when we are exhausted from trying to fix our problems by ourselves, do we get to the place where we finally say, "Okay, God. I need you."

God should be the first one we turn to when we are facing an issue, just like a parent/child relationship. Before we act, we must go to God.

When we finally do turn to God, His response is, "You should have come to me in the first place. I am still going to help you, but you would have saved yourself from additional problems if you would have come to me in the first place."

God should be the first one we turn to when we are facing an issue, just like a parent/child relationship. Parents expect their children to turn to them first in times of trouble no matter their age. Before we act, we must go to God. My grown children still come to me with questions wanting advice before they make a decision because they value my wisdom and experience. We must value the knowledge of God and revere His position as our Father.

I do not care how old my children get, I do not want them to call me, "Michael." I want them to call me, "Daddy." This title describes our relationship and reinforces that I am not simply a friend, but their father who loves them. This is the kind of closeness we should strive for with our Father in Heaven. We must always recognize who we are, who He is, and how our relationship with Him is structured. He is our Father and we are His children.

When I was a Child, I Thought like a Child

*So do not be like them; for your Father knows what you need before you ask Him. — **Matthew 6:8***

Jesus said when we go to God, He already knows what we need. Clearly, when we pray, we do not tell God anything that He does not already know. It is not as if God hears our prayers and says, "Wait a minute, I did not know that!" However, praying shows God that we have humbled ourselves and are willing to turn to Him.

As such, praying is an act of submission.

We cannot submit however, if we try to control the outcome of our prayer. If God knows everything, then why do we tell Him how to work our situations out? We say, "God, I need you to help me in this situation." As soon as God begins to work, we say, "No God, not that way." And God responds, "You have to let me work it out."

Why? Because God can see our life from beginning to end, whereas, we can only see one day at a time.

He knows what's best for us.

This is no different from my children, Sharia, Michael, Ciara and Joshua, when they were younger, saying to me, "Dad, why do I have to learn algebra? I am not going to be a math major." What they did not realize was, math teaches basic thinking skills, which can be applied to any job. In fact advanced mathematics is actually called logic, because it teaches you how to process thoughts and solve problems. I told them, "If you ever want to be in management on a job, you have to learn how to think logically and assess problems accurately.

God, in the same way, says, "You have to go through some difficult situations that may not seem to be beneficial at the moment. I know you do not like it. I know you are mad. I know you are upset. I know your heart is broken. But my child, I have to let you go through these situations, because the lessons learned now will help you down the road. Then when the blessings come, you are going to thank Me that you went through periods of testing and struggle."

Power and Trust

We have to learn to trust God in every situation, and not just when it is convenient. We have to trust Him when it is painful, when we are frustrated, when we are alone, and when we are upset. Why? Because the Lord knows how to direct our paths.

> Trust in the Lord with all your heart and do not lean on your own understanding. In all your ways acknowledge Him, and He will make your paths straight. — **Proverbs 3:5-6**

When we trust God and follow Him, He leads us where we have to go. He loves us and wants us to ask Him for help, but we have to swallow our pride and say, "God, I need you. I cannot do this by myself. I am struggling. My flesh, my finances, my family, my friends, whatever it is God, I need you to move in my situation."

There was a great preacher during the 1800s named Charles Finney. He was an evangelist who would go to metropolitan cities and preach to several thousand people. During these services hundreds of people would be saved.

Someone once asked him, "What is the power in your preaching?" He replied, "The power is not in my preaching, but in the prayer behind the preaching." He went on to explain that while he was travelling and preaching the gospel, his partner, Daniel Nash would rent a hotel room in the city where Finney would be going and do nothing but fast and pray for a week prior to the revival. Daniel prayed that God would soften the hearts of the people who would attend and have their spirits ready to the point that when the word came forth, they would cry out, "What must I do to be saved?"

It is not just our worship or our attendance on Sunday mornings—it is our prayer life that helps us grow as individuals, as ministries, and as the body of Christ.

He concluded his answer by saying, "The power is not in my preaching, but the power is in prayer."

Another evangelist, Billy Graham did not think he was a great preacher. He said, "We always focused our prayers on the altar call." And he said all those thousands of people who came to Christ "did not come just because of my preaching, but they came because people were praying."

It is not just our worship or our attendance on Sunday mornings that helps us grow and become more like Christ. Rather it is our *prayer life* that helps us grow as individuals, as churches, and as the body of Christ. If it is our desire to look more like Christ, then we should follow His example and let prayer be the foundation of our Christian life.

WORKBOOK

Chapter One Questions

Question: What can we learn from the amount of prayer in Jesus' life? How does it compare to your prayer life?

_____

_____

_____

_____

_____

_____

_____

_____

_____

_____

_____

_____

_____

_____

_____

Question: In what ways are your prayers ritualistic? How are they relational?

_____

_____

_____

_____

_____

_____

_____

_____

_____

_____

_____

_____

_____

_____

Question: How does it feel to consider God in the intimate role of Daddy in your life?

_____

_____

_____

_____

_____

_____

_____

_____

_____

_____

_____

_____

_____

_____

_____

_____

Action: God is not afraid of your feelings. He wants you to be real with Him. This means telling Him exactly how you are feeling, even if that is a feeling of anger, disappointment, or frustration. He is God, and He can handle it. He is the creator of your every emotion, and not a single one is a surprise to Him. Trust in Him to be not only your Heavenly Father, but also your Abba or Daddy. As a child runs toward a parent after a long day at school, run to your Father and tell him of your sorrows and exasperation. Stop praying prayers out of ritual and repetition. He knows the words of those prayers, and He knows what you need, but He longs to hear it from your heart and not your memory. Purpose today that you will give Him the relationship with you that He desires. Decide to put away the prayers of the past, and bring to Him a new song of your soul—one of gratitude, praise, and honesty.

Notes

CHAPTER TWO

Getting from "What You Want" to "What God Wants"

"...not My will, but Yours, be done."— ***Luke 22:42***

It is in our prayers that we fellowship, commune, and become intimate with God. As mentioned in chapter 1, Jesus never said, "If you pray", He said, "When you pray." There is an expectation that prayer is to be a part of our daily lives.

Oftentimes, we recite the Lord's Prayer, but how much of this prayer do we really understand? At times people will say things but do not fully grasp what they are saying. For example, when a couple gets married, do they comprehend the full scope of what they're promising in their vows?

They stand up and vow to love each other, "For richer or for poorer, in good times and bad times, in sickness and in health until death do us part." I have married many couples who take this vow and say, "I do" yet when poor, bad, and sick times come their answer changes to "I don't." In reality what they meant at their wedding was, "I will love you in richer, in good times and in health." They did not perceive the depth of the vow they were making.

When it comes to prayer, we often say things because they sound spiritual. However, like wedding vows, we really do not understand the extent or the ramifications of what we are saying. With that in mind, let's take a look at the next phrase in the Lord's Prayer - "Your kingdom come, your will be done." Matthew 6:10

Your Kingdom Come

In order to have a kingdom there must be a king. When there is a king, the king has absolute rule. In a monarchy, or a kingdom ruled by a king, the king has the first, the last, and the only say. Whatever the king says goes.

However, when it comes to our relationship with God, we often operate with an American democratic mindset which says: everything has to be fair and I have to have a vote. When we bring this mindset to God, it looks a little something like this: "Okay God, let me know your plans for my life and I will let you know if I agree with what you have planned."

We live our physical lives in a political democracy but our spiritual lives are not controlled by the same democracy. In fact, our spiritual lives are as far from a political democracy as possible. If we call ourselves

Christians then we live in a theocracy, or a kingdom ruled by God. Historically, kings & queens had an obligation to rule the land and to protect the people that lived within the monarch's realm. Their subjects, or the people within their realm, did what the kings and queens told them to do. This is how it worked for centuries, and this is the pattern God has for us. He is our king and we are His subjects.

We want the benefits of being connected to the king and living under His protection but we do not want to serve Him or submit ourselves to His rules. We will often only serve God as long as we agree with what He is doing in our lives and gives us what we want.

We will pray:

- "God, have your way in my life,' but add "as long as I agree with it."

- "God, do what you have to do," and caution "as long as it doesn't hurt."

- "God, I want you to make my life brand-new," but hope "as long as nothing bad happens to me."

We may not pray these prayers word for word, but in our minds and hearts we are saying, "Father, I want my will to be done, not yours." To fully enjoy our relationship with God we must shed our selfish nature and embrace the will of the King for our lives.

Having a Kingdom Mentality

Many of Jesus' parables give examples of a kingdom mentality. A kingdom mentality is when we have committed our lives to God and seek to fulfill His will on earth. One attribute of this mentality will cause us to value the people that He values: the least, the less and the lost. With this mentality we will love our neighbor as ourselves, be our brother's keeper, encourage one another, lift up one another, and bear one another's burdens. Kingdom is recognizing God's desire for each person to live in relationship and submission to Him. In His parables and in His life Jesus demonstrated that every person has value to God.

Jesus could have been born at any time and within any social or political realm he wanted. Why did God choose His son to be born to a poor and homeless Hebrew woman? Because God wanted to identify with the poor and oppressed, and say that they have just as much value to God as the wealthy. Jesus spent much of His ministry time with the outcasts to show that God loves them as much as He loves anybody. Often, those we reject are the ones that God wants us to reach with His message of love.

Many of us struggle with having a kingdom mentality because we only want to interact with individuals who look, act and believe just like us. Some of us think we have cornered the market on following God. Jesus's disciple felt the same way. In Luke 9:49-50 John says to Jesus, "Master, we saw someone casting out demons in

Your name; and we tried to prevent him because he does not follow along with us." But Jesus said to him, "Do not hinder him; for he who is not against you is for you." There are other Christians who may not worship or pray like us but they are just as important to God. Thinking like God causes us to see the value in everyone not just in ourselves.

Having a kingdom mentality means that we truly want God's kingdom to come and His will to be done.

Another attribute of the kingdom mentality, recognizes that God's desire is to get the glory out of everything we go through. When we encounter difficult situations He wants our focus to be on Him and not the situation. Having a kingdom mentality means that we truly want God's kingdom to come and His will to be done. We have to submit and line up with the desire of our king. God wants us to want things His way, as in "Not my will, Lord, but your will be done."

A Battle of the Wills

Have you ever engaged in a battle of wills with God? When you had to make a decision, did you make up your mind first and go to God looking for Him to approve of your decision? Did you make your decision before you asked whether it was His will or not? Perhaps your prayer sounded something like this:

"It's a good opportunity, God, please show me if it's your will." But you pray this after you have already made up your mind. Perhaps you have said "God he seems like a good Christian man and I really like him but show me if he is the one for me." However you pray this after you have been intimate with him.

When we make up our minds and then go to God, we create a situation where we want God to submit to our will instead of the other way around. When we do this, we are playing a dangerous game with God because we, in our limited understanding, play the role of God and assume we know more than Him. We should not play this game with God. Do not say, "God, I want your will to come, as long as I agree with it." Instead we need to use the example of Jesus. Jesus is the perfect example of submitting to God's will. In the garden of Gethsemane, before the soldiers came to arrest Him, Jesus asked His father if there was a way for the sin debt to be paid without Him having to die. Jesus, though did not stay in this questioning state. He continued, "Nevertheless, not my will but Your will be done."

When we pray for God's will to be done, we must accept everything that happens as part of His divine plan. We just have to accept His will. Trying to negotiate with God is not an option. The prophet Jeremiah found this out the hard way. He struggled with doing God's will and proclaiming judgment against the nation of Israel. He decided that he would not speak anymore but God's word was as a fire in his belly. He finally acquiesced and in chapter 20:7 he said, *"You are stronger than I, and You have prevailed."* He learned as we learn, that God's will is going to come to pass and that total submission is what He requires.

Two Kinds of Wills

God has two kinds of wills: His permissive will and His divine will. God's permissive will is when we keep asking for something so much that God allows us to have it in order to teach us a lesson. God's divine will is when we are right in the center of where God wants us and has directed us to be. In eighth chapter of 1 Samuel, the nation of Israel wanted to be like the other nations, so they requested that Samuel appoint a king to rule over them. However, it was not God's divine will for the nation to have a human king rule over them because He wanted to rule over them. God told Samuel, "Listen to the people and everything they say to you. They have not rejected you; they have rejected Me as their king...you must solemnly warn them and tell them about the rights of the king who will rule over them." When Samuel told the Nation of Israel God's response, which also included a warning, they insisted on having a king. Therefore, the Lord finally said in response to their request, "Listen to them, appoint a king for them." God knew what was best for the people, but since they strongly desired a king He gave them one. In the end it came with a hefty price because the Nation of Israel was actually rejecting God's rule. Beginning with King Saul, the Israelites experienced difficulty and defeat because they were no longer in God's divine will.

Like the Nation of Israel, God will let us have the very things we continually ask for. He tries to warn us when what we ask for is not in His divine will, because often times the result of what we want will cause more pain than comfort. God wants us to realize that He knows what we need more than we do. Unfortunately, many of us do not come to this realization until after we are outside of His will, and what we wanted has caused so much hurt and pain. Once we have received what we begged God for and then consequently experience trouble and affliction that is when God picks us up, just like He did with the nation of Israel. Even when we step out of His divine will, He still loves us enough to pick us back up and place us where we should be - broken pieces and all.

Once we are back in His divine will, God wants us to listen for His voice regarding all future decisions. We need to make the decision that if we do not hear His voice concerning our request, then we are going to stand still and wait until He tells us what to do. The irony of being in God's divine will is that we will still experience difficulties. However, these difficulties are not due to our rejection of God but for our perfection in Christ. There will be storms that are designed for the sole purpose of making us look more like Jesus. This is God's divine will.

God does not want us to die in our spiritual storms, so He equips us to handle the storms of life. God gives us everything we need to persevere in the midst of the storm because He says, "I need you to get through this so that you understand that I know better than you."

Without fail, when we try to survive life's storms in our own strength and without God, we will perish and die. In the midst of the storm our prayer should be, "Lord, as long as you keep me, I am going to make it through this storm."

God strengthens us is by letting us go through tough difficult circumstances and then He graciously delivers us to remind us He is in control. David said, in much more poetic terms, in Psalm 23, "Even when I go through the darkest valley, I fear no danger, for You are with me."

We might pray prayers and sing songs like:

- I want Your kingdom to come.

- I want Your spirit to move

- I want Your anointing to fall like fire

- I want You to move in my life

Are we willing to do whatever it takes for that to happen? For God's kingdom to come, there will be struggle. For His Spirit to move, we will be humbled. For his anointing to fall like fire, there must be sacrifice. For God to move in our lives, we must be obedient to His will. Are we truly prepared for and desire, "Thy kingdom come, Thy will be done" Do we discipline ourselves for the coming kingdom? Do we deny ourselves for God's will to reign over us? We must! Because when we do things God's way, circumstances always work out.

Each one of us was born with a divine purpose and destiny, but we have to line ourselves up with God's will in order to obtain it. In Romans, Paul says that when we search the mind of the spirit, we will discover the will of God and begin to operate within the will of God.

> *Delight yourself in the Lord and He will give you the desires of your heart.* — **Psalms 37:4**

In Hebrew, the word "delight" means to be pliable or moldable, which means to allow God to mold us to His will. When that happens, *you want* what *He wants*.

So I challenge you to pray, "Lord, do what you have to do to bring Your divine will to pass in my life. I submit myself to you, have your way in my life." By offering up your life to God, you give Him permission to interrupt your life and you concede your will to His divine will.

WORKBOOK

Chapter Two Questions

Question: When you pray, do you fully understand your prayers? Are you repeating words that hold meaning within your heart and reflect your desires in speaking with God, or are you reciting something memorized?

_____

_____

_____

_____

_____

_____

_____

_____

_____

_____

_____

_____

_____

_____

_____

Question: Are you praying with the mindset of spiritual democracy? Are you hesitant to accept a kingdom mentality? How might this be affecting the way in which God can work in your life?

_____

_____

_____

_____

_____

_____

_____

_____

_____

_____

_____

_____

Question: How can you embrace the will of the King in your prayer life? What prayers would you include to this end?

_____

_____

_____

_____

_____

_____

_____

_____

_____

_____

_____

_____

_____

_____

_____

Question: Can you think of a time when you experienced God's permissive will? What did you learn from that time?

_____

_____

_____

_____

_____

_____

_____

_____

_____

_____

_____

_____

_____

_____

_____

Action: When we are in the correct posture of submission and obedience to God, we understand that in order to be in His will fully, we must include Him in all areas of our life. This means that we must ask Him for His opinion before we decide what our own is. His opinion might not align with what we were hoping for; however, we can be confident and assured that it is for our best. Storms and struggles are part of life, and we are called to endure them in His name. We can be confident that He will walk before us every time. God sees the big picture, all of the details, and the effects of every decision we make. He has cared for you from your first breath, and He can see your last, so trust Him. Stop negotiating with God and trying to bend His will to match your own. You do not want to live in His permissible will; you want to live in His divine will. Align and mold your desires with His, and reach your full spiritual potential, delighting yourself in Him.

Notes

_____

_____

_____

_____

_____

_____

_____

_____

_____

_____

_____

_____

_____

_____

_____

_____

_____

_____

_____

_____

_____

_____

_____

CHAPTER THREE

Nutritious Daily Bread

Then the Lord said to Moses, 'Behold, I will rain bread from heaven for you; and the people shall go out and gather a day's portion every day, that I may test them, whether or not they will walk in My instruction.' —
Exodus 16:4

The previous chapter presented the idea that God's divine will does not allow tough situations to come to destroy us but to mature us. He uses arduous and toilsome trials to position us in a place of complete trust. If we could endure struggles on our own, then we would feel that we do not need God. If we had the ability, the know-how, and the intellect to get through trying situations, we would not need Him. But we do not have the ability nor are we strong enough to stand on our own. Since we do not have the strength, God will put us in a places where we have nothing but Him, because then we will depend on Him.

Of course, we always want to know the "whys", the "whens", and the "wheres" when it comes to the will of

God especially when going through tough times. We do not like it when God withholds the full plan He has for us. He expects us to trust Him completely. It is while trusting Him that God provides for our needs as we live out His plan for our lives. When relying on His provision we are allowing God, and nothing else, to sustain us.

"Give us today our daily bread", or as some early translations say, "Give us today our necessary bread." This is the first time in the Lord's Prayer where Christ asks something of God.

We treat God like Santa Clause: "Lord, I want you to do this and please give me this." Where is the element of worship? Where is the element of praise?

Why is this significant? When teaching His disciples to pray, Jesus did not begin the prayer with a petition. How often do we begin our prayers by automatically asking something of God? We seek His provision before we seek Him. We treat God like Santa Clause: "Lord, I want you to do this and please give me this." Where is the element of worship? Where is the element of praise? Where is the aspect of our relationship with Him?

Petitioning God and asking for His help is not wrong. After all, Jesus Himself did so. However there is a way that we should ask. Jesus started the prayer proclaiming His relationship with God and then followed up with the worship of God. When Christ prayed for daily bread, He asked God to fill a need but only after worship. Bread is sustenance for the body but worship is necessary for the soul.

After worship is when we ask for the bread. Within the Jewish culture bread was frequently used during meal time. It was easy to make and wheat was readily available. Wheat could grow even in the arid landscape of Israel, Egypt, and Palestine, so it was a common part of every meal. Just like that bread met a physical need God too wants to meet our physical needs today.

God's desire is to provide for each and every one of our needs. Unfortunately, everyone is not going to live in Beverly Hills with a house in Malibu. Nor is every person going to drive a luxury car. We have to understand that there is a place where our needs and wants intersect. This is the place where God will give us what we need but not necessarily what we want. For example, a person needs a car and wants a Mercedes Benz. However, God provides that person with the resources to get a Toyota Camry. He has not given them the provision for what they want but provision for what they need. That person can reject God's provision and get the car they cannot afford risking repossession and not having a car at all or accept His provision and easily afford the car God has provided the resources for them to obtain. This does not mean that you will never have the Benz. As we demonstrate thankfulness for His provision we set ourselves up to receive greater blessing down the road.

We must always have an attitude of thankfulness for God's provision even when we do not get what we want.

Have we been guilty of thinking one of the following thoughts?

- I have a refrigerator full of food, but I have nothing to eat.

- I have a job, but I don't like it.

- I have money, but not enough.

- I have a closet full of clothes, but I have nothing to wear.

Unfortunately, we often have an unappreciative attitude when it comes to God's provision. The result of our ungrateful demeanor towards God prevents us from growing closer to Him on a daily basis because when praying for our needs, we misunderstand the meaning of daily bread.

Praying for Today

Martin Luther, the great leader of the Reformation, wrote: "What does daily bread mean? Everything that nourishes our body and meets its needs such as food, drink, clothing, shoes, house, yard, fields, cattle, money, possessions, a devout spouse, devout children, devout employees, devout and faithful rulers, good government, good weather, peace, health, discipline, honor, good friends, faithful neighbors and other things like these."

Martin Luther is stressing to the reader that daily bread is more than just physical food. Clearly daily bread represents the things we need every day.

> *In our current culture, we really miss out on the present because our minds are so fixated on what is going to happen in the future. That is why Jesus reminds us not to worry about tomorrow since it has enough problems of its own.*

Keeping that in mind, what should we pray for on a daily basis? Clearly, daily bread is anything that meets a need and impacts us on a daily basis. We can pray for our children, our spouse, the church, our local, state, and national leaders, and the communities in which we live. We can also pray that God gives us whatever it is we need *today*.

In our current culture, many miss out on the present because of the fixation on what may happen in the future. We should be reminded of Jesus's word when He said, "Therefore don't worry about tomorrow, because tomorrow will worry about itself." One clear example of this idea is found early in the Bible.

When the children of Israel came out of Egypt, they were in the wilderness without any food. Mercifully, God allowed manna to fall from heaven to nourish the people. This wheat-like substance was found on the ground in the morning dew, and they would gather it, crush it, and make bread to eat. The Lord told them to collect only enough to eat for the day, and any attempt at gathering more for storage would result in the excess turning to worms.

Some people did not believe what God said and they tried to collect all the manna they could. As a result, the next day, all the unused manna turned into worms. Why would God, who is so loving and gracious, allow their food to turn into worms? Because He wanted them to depend on Him daily to provide for them.

Our daily bread is not only what we need materialistically—it also helps us grow in our relationship with God every single day.

God wants *us* to depend on Him daily as well. That is the lesson of the manna.

This applies to prayer as well. Jesus had an expectation that we would pray to God daily. God doesn't expect us to pray only when a loved one is sick, when a family member is incarcerated, when we are looking for a job, when we have been fighting with our spouse or when our children are getting on our nerves. We are expected to pray *daily*. When we pray for our daily bread, we not only get what we need materialistically but it also helps us grow in our relationship with God every single day.

What we find is that God cares about all our needs. In Matthew chapter 15, there is a story where Jesus was with His disciples, and a woman came running after them, shouting at Him and making a scene. She hollered, "Jesus, my daughter is filled with a demonic spirit, please touch her." Jesus responded to her, "I cannot give the children's bread unto dogs." He said this because she was not a Jew. Jesus was actually setting the stage to demonstrate to His disciples that God cares for the needs of everyone.

The woman responded, "Yes, but even the dogs eat the crumbs that fall from the master's table." She was basically saying, "I don't need the whole loaf of bread, just give me some crumbs to feed me today." This is an attitude that appreciates the daily provision that God gives.

If we desire to live the Lord's Prayer, then we must be in the habit of praying for others and in doing so we demonstrate love for our neighbor.

Furthermore, this is the mentality we must have with the Lord. We need to be content with saying, "God, you don't have to pay all my bills, but give me enough to make it through today. I might not know what I am going to eat tomorrow, but give me enough food to make it through today." This mentality demonstrates that we completely trust God to provide for us daily.

Our needs are obviously important, but they should not be our only focus. Not only should we pray for our needs but also for the needs of others. When Jesus prayed He did not say, "Give me today *my* daily bread." He said, "Give us today *our* daily bread. The request Jesus makes is one that is concerned for the needs of others. Our desire should not be for God to bless only us and not anyone else. We must have a concern for others and petition God to meet their needs as well. If we take Martin Luther's description of daily bread to heart, we must unite in prayer with others around us even when their need is not our need. If we desire to live the Lord's Prayer then we must be in the habit of praying for others and in doing so we demonstrate love for our neighbor.

Spiritual Hunger

Another aspect of receiving our daily bread is reading and digesting the Word of God. The Word of God is metaphorically called bread. Additionally, Jesus is described as *the bread of life.* This presupposes that we need both prayer and the word of God on a daily basis to sustain us spiritually. It is detrimental to our Christian walk when we are physically satisfied but spiritually devoid of God's word. When we are not in the habit of spending time with the Lord and consuming His word, we are prone to substitute His word with worldly things that appeal to us. These worldly things are like candy, they may taste sweet but have no nutritional value, and if we consume too much we will become sick.

Psychologists say we should never go grocery shopping when we are hungry—we will not think clearly, and will make poor food choices. Everything will look appealing and we will wind up grabbing groceries that are not necessarily healthy for us. It works the same way spiritually.

When we are spiritually starved, we begin looking for ways to fill that gnawing void with spiritual junk food. This junk food is anything that takes focus off the Lord. Too often, Christians substitute daily bread for daily junk. Because we are bombarded everyday with spiritual junk food we need to be intentional about what we feed our spirit. In the end, daily bread is important, because you are what you eat.

Giving Thanks for the Daily Bread

Finally, God expects us to be thankful for our daily bread. There is nothing worse than giving someone something they are not thankful for. Think about it: How many times has God blessed us and we did not take the time to thank Him? We have all been there.

He wants us to be thankful for the daily bread. We might not have everything that we want, but He gives us everything that we need, and we need to be grateful for His daily provision.

God does things in our lives that we will never understand. We get upset, start complaining, and all the while God is being our Daddy, saying to us: "You do not understand the nutrients and the blessings that are in this food."

As most parents know, children often do not like to eat vegetables, they would much rather have Doritos, Twinkies or some other snack. What do parents say to this kind of request? A typical parent, like myself, would say "No! You need to eat your vegetables." Why? Because we understand how the nutrients in the foods benefit our children and aid in their growth. But our children do not understand benefits yet.

Similarly, God does things in our lives and often we do not see the benefits. We get upset and start complaining, all the while God is being our Daddy, saying to us:

"You do not understand the nutrients and the blessings that are in this food." When it comes to God's provision, we must trust Him for it, thank Him when we receive, savor it when we eat it, and anticipate Him giving us more the next day.

WORKBOOK

Chapter Three Questions

Question: How is worship a part of your prayer life? Do you only make requests or do you also thank God for what He has already done as well?

_____

_____

_____

_____

_____

_____

_____

_____

_____

_____

_____

_____

_____

_____

Question: What would you list as your daily bread? What are your needs, and how has God met them?

_____

_____

_____

_____

_____

_____

_____

_____

_____

_____

_____

_____

_____

Question: What percentage of your prayers are for yourself? What percentage is for others? How might you need to adjust your prayer life in this regard?

_____

_____

_____

_____
_____
_____
_____
_____
_____
_____
_____
_____
_____
_____
_____
_____
_____

Question: Are you spiritually hungry? How do you feed your spirit every day with God's Word?

_____
_____
_____
_____
_____
_____
_____
_____
_____
_____
_____
_____
_____

_____

_____

_____

Action: Decide today to include God's Word in your daily life. Just as you commit to eating breakfast, lunch, and dinner, commit also to feeding your spirit. The enemy will find every way to keep you too busy, forgetful, or complacent to spend time nourishing your spirit with truth. You must commit yourself to a daily practice of reading God's Word, talking with Him, and being aware of the ways that the enemy will try to distract you from feeding yourself in this way. Pray for God to make you aware of the times you are being starved spiritually. Trust Him for your spiritual nutrition. He knows exactly what your soul needs to be fed and to thrive. We serve a faithful and loving God who will meet your needs tomorrow, just as He has today. As a loving parent, God has provided for His children since He created them. Adam and Eve did not have every single thing they wanted, but every need was met. Talk to God about your needs and wants. Ask Him to reveal the difference between the two. He will always provide for His children, and He is faithful to continue meeting your needs forever. Rest in that knowledge, and find peace in His provision.

Notes

CHAPTER FOUR

What it Means to Forgive

In the last few chapters we have learned the important aspects of prayer that need to be present in our daily lives – reverence, praise and it does not end there. Jesus now stresses the importance of forgiveness.

Forgive us our debts as we forgive our debtors. —**Matthew 6:12**

For if you forgive other people when they sin against you, your heavenly Father will also forgive you. —**Matthew 6:14**

When we forgive we give up the right to retaliate against a person for the wrong that they have committed against us. In this passage Jesus does not begin by saying, "Forgive those who did us wrong." Rather He begins by saying, "Forgive us our debts." That word *debt* in the Greek could also be translated as "sin" or "trespass." In Luke's account, He says, "Forgive us our trespasses as we forgive those who trespassed against us." A more literal translation would be this: "Forgive us our sins as we forgive those who have sinned against us."

Forgiveness is the apex of what God did through Jesus Christ. When we were still sinners, God sent His Son to pay the price for sin by dying on the cross. The shedding of His blood was for the forgiveness of our sins. Therefore we, as Christians, must be willing to forgive others just as much as God has forgiven us. However, before we can forgive others, we first have to acknowledge that we need to be forgiven. In order to do this, we must first recognize our sins, humble ourselves, and go to God with a spirit of repentance, asking Him to forgive us.

Sin is not something we learn how to do, we are born with that nature. Children do not have to be taught how to be selfish, to lie or be disobedient. It just comes naturally. Sin became our nature after the fall of Adam and Eve in the Garden of Eden. They disobeyed God's command, sin became man's nature and the effect was felt instantaneously.

When God confronted Adam in the Garden of Eden, He asked him if he had sinned. Adam responded, not by asking for forgiveness, but by blaming God. Adam said in essence, God, that woman you gave me, the one I didn't even ask for, it was her fault.

And then the woman in turn said, God, it was not my fault either. It was the snake.

We are still perpetuating the same behavior today. We attempt to justify sinful behavior by saying, "It was not my fault. If that person did not push me the way they did, I would not have reacted the way I did." Or, "If that person would not have said what they said, I would not have cursed them out."

When we ask for forgiveness and repent, we are not blaming others nor are we trying to justify our actions to alleviate our guilt. True repentance says, "God, please forgive me. I, and I alone am guilty because I handled that situation wrong."

After Christ teaches that we need to ask God to forgive us, He continues by saying that we should forgive those who have sinned against us.

This is an area where many Christians struggle. We often do not want to forgive other people. We want to hold on to their wrongdoings. We do not want to forgive them because deep down (or maybe not so deep down), we think we can have power over that person and manipulate them through guilt. We think that controlling the situation will make us feel better, but we are missing what God is trying to do when we will not forgive them. We need to forgive others and not just ask God to forgive us.

This is an area where many Christians struggle. We often do not want to forgive other people. We want to hold onto their wrongdoings.

When repenting, the confession to God says, "Lord, I have sinned and I was wrong. I have disobeyed your word and I ask that you to forgive me." When we ask

God to forgive us He will because of Christ. Who are we to then think we are too big to forgive someone else when they do something wrong to us? This attitude says, "God, I am bigger than You."

How can we expect God to forgive us, but we will not forgive others? Think about the level of audacity and arrogance in that statement. As soon as somebody does something wrong to us we think, "That's it, I'm not going to talk to them anymore. I never want to speak to them again." We do this at work, in relationships, and especially in the church, but we have to learn how to forgive. If every time we sinned God cut us off, we would be all alone.

Matthew 6:14 provides further teaching about the importance of forgiving: "For if you forgive people their wrong doing, your father in heaven will forgive you, but if you don't forgive them, your father will not forgive you." This is one of those verses we do not like to talk about, but God meant what He said. We must learn how to forgive others. Why? Because that's what Jesus did for us. He forgives us for our wrongdoings so we in turn need to forgive others. His forgiveness is not conditional so neither can our forgiveness be conditional. Jesus tells us in no uncertain terms that we will only be forgiven as we forgive others.

People say, "I will forgive you, but I am not going to forget what you did." God addresses this argument in Isaiah 1:18, which says, "Though your sins be as scarlet I will make them white as snow and I will blot out your every transgression." Forgetting is an act of the will. We may not be able to physically erase the hurt and trauma, but we have a choice whether to dwell on it or to let it go.

> *Every time the devil wants to throw your past up in your face, you need to say, "Stop, my sin is covered by the blood."*

The same way we choose to love, we have to choose to forgive and choose not to remember. In Isaiah, the Lord says that when He forgives us, He casts our sins into the sea of forgetfulness. It does not disappear in the sea—the Lord just does not go deep sea diving and bring it back up. Choosing to move past a situation and let it go, is key to restoration and reconciliation.

Some of our strongest relationships were born out of the act of forgiveness. One problem we face today is that we do not want to work through our problems. People will hurt us and betray our trust then we will spend years avoiding that person instead of forgiving and moving on.

Whenever there has been a violation of trust in a relationship, and the other party apologizes we need to forgive them. Their apology indicates their willingness to begin the process of restoration. Our forgiveness says, "I am willing to work with you in that process of restoration." Trust can only be restored when there has been both apology and forgiveness.

Forgiveness then becomes a pillar upon which this restored trust rests. If we cannot forgive and get past the actions of another, then the relationship and the trust will never be restored.

In our litigious society, where the focus is usually more concerned with lawsuits and conflict than with restoration, we often will not forgive if we feel that our point of view is right. We will hold out our righteousness as a banner of victory. However, we can further damage relationships to the point of disrepair by proving that we are right. When there is an offense, God is not as concerned with who is right or wrong as He is with restoration and reconciliation. God is so concerned with restoration and reconciliation that He sent Jesus to die to restore our relationship with Him.

We are guilty, but God does not point fingers at our guilt. He simply reminds us that His Son died for our sins and that His blood washes us clean.

True forgiveness is not even about the person we forgive, it is about our relationship with God and Him doing a transformative work in our heart and in our spirit. When our relationship with God is right, He fills our hearts with His love to the point that we have the ability to forgive and love others like Christ has loved us. When this happens, we will not only see ourselves as the image of God but we will see His image in others too.

When we are unable to forgive others, it is often because we do not see His image in ourselves and we believe that God has not forgiven us. God created us to be filled with His love and experience His forgiveness. When we cannot forgive someone else, it is many times a result of our own inability to forgive ourselves.

The first time we came to the altar and asked God to forgive us, He washed us clean forever.

We often go to God repeatedly, week after week, repenting for the same thing, asking Him to forgive us again and again. This is because guilt and shame have clouded our minds and we think we are not forgiven. This is a trick of the enemy who wants to keep us from experiencing all that God has for us. However, in 1 John 1:9 the writer says, "If we confess our sins He is faithful and just to forgive us and to cleanse us from all unrighteousness." The first time we went to the altar and sincerely repented and asked God to forgive us, the blood of Jesus washed us clean forever.

It is easy to tell when individuals have been through difficult situations and have forgiven themselves for their failures. They usually have more compassion than those who has never experienced difficulty. We have to embrace this truth and learn to love and forgive ourselves. When we are able to forgive ourselves for the wrongs we have done, we are then able to forgive others.

The Danger of Not Forgiving

Another reason to forgive is because un-forgiveness keeps us bound to the person and the action that caused us damage. If we see that person on the street we are mentally and emotionally drawn back to the incident, no matter how much time has passed. It takes a lot of emotion to stay angry and not forgive. We waste energy trying to remember who lied to us, who stole from us and who treated us wrong. Doing so is pointless because often those individuals have moved on and are living their lives having a good time. They are not thinking about us and sometimes do not even know we are still angry. Ultimately forgiving those persons sets us free from having to hold on to hurt and pain. Un-forgiveness also can hinder our relationship with God.

In 1 Peter 3:7, the Apostle Peter says that when there are unresolved issues between husbands and wives and they are unforgiving toward one another, the Lord does not hear their prayers. This should serve as additional motivation to forgive others and not stay angry. If we are expected to communicate with God everyday through prayer, we should remove as many hindrances as possible.

When we encounter people who have mistreated us, we should not think: "I don't know why they are happy after the way they treated me, they should be ashamed of themselves." Instead, pray: "God, bless their lives. Keep them and cover them. Draw them closer to you and make a difference in their lives." We should pray for those persons who have mistreated us and hurt us. Jesus said in Matthew 5:44 "…love your enemies, and pray for those who persecute you."

Think about it this way: If the only way for God to bless me is for me to pray for somebody else, then I'm going to pray for every last one of my haters because the truth is, it is the people who are hating on me that help push me to where I am today. Do not stay angry with anyone. In fact we can thank those people who hurt us and pushed us closer to God.

My faith is as strong as it is today because of those individuals who forced me to seek God's face. I can honestly say that I have forgiven people who never acknowledged their wrongdoing or apologized to me. Although initially not a simple task, I learned that my relationship with God and my capacity for love and happiness all increased when I was not focused on past hurts.

Forgive Them Anyway

When a person, either because of pride or apathy, refuses to apologize for a wrongdoing, our heart should still be positioned to forgive. We must be willing to forgive others because all of us are guilty of sinning and not always acknowledging it. As we discussed earlier, each of us was born with a sinful nature and we are reminded that un-forgiveness of others hinders us from receiving God's blessings. We need to learn how to forgive people who have wronged us and who never apologize.

In the book of Job, Job's friends treated him in an unfriendly manner. They talked negatively to him and accused him of being a sinner. After several chapters of his friends attacking his character and his personhood, God comes to Job in chapter 42 and says, I'm angry with your friends, but I'm so angry with them that I do not even want them to pray to me. I want you to pray for them that I will forgive them.

Jobs prayed for his friends and God gave him back a double amount of everything he had lost. I have heard many preachers preach Job chapter 42 and focus on Job receiving double the amount he lost. To me the greater point is, although Job did indeed receive double, it was only after he prayed for his friends. He prayed for the same people who treated him wrongly, asking God to forgive them and bless them. To pray this type of prayer, it is evident that Job had to first forgive them for their treatment of him. Nowhere in this text did his friends ever ask for forgiveness or apologize. God will restore what we have lost, but we must first learn to forgive those who have wronged us. Like Job, that restoration may ultimately bring us more than what was formally in our possession.

WORKBOOK

Chapter Four Questions

Question: Do you see the need in your life for God's forgiveness? How has His forgiveness changed your life and the way you live?

_____

_____

Question: Whom in your life do you need to forgive? What is holding you back from doing so? Have you spoken with God about it?

_____

_____

_____

_____

_____

_____

_____

_____

_____

_____

_____

_____

_____

_____

Question: Why do you think forgiveness is included in the Lord's Prayer? Why should we choose to forgive?

_____

_____

_____

_____

_____

_____

_____

_____

_____

_____

_____

_____

_____

_____

_____

_____

Question: Who could use your prayers right now, even if they have hurt you?

_____

_____

_____

_____

_____

_____

_____

_____

_____

_____

_____

_____

_____

_____

Action: Forgiveness is a choice we make, not a feeling. If you are waiting to feel forgiving towards someone, wait no more. Choose to forgive this person with the faith and knowledge that it is what Jesus has commanded us to do, in order to be forgiven ourselves. God wants us to forgive one another because it is good for us. It frees us of the chains of bitterness that surround our hearts when we harbor remembrance of past wrongdoings.

Make the choice today to set bitterness free and forgive. Fill your heart with the truth that you are forgiven through His holy sacrifice. Ask Him to take your bitterness and replace it with love. He is faithful to answer and provide. If you struggle to move past the feelings that prevent you from truly releasing your anger and bitterness, pray about it. God sees all, and He is well aware of how you've been hurt, and by whom. You can share your deepest hurts and pain with your Heavenly Father.

Forgiveness is at the center of God's heart. It is important to Him, and so it should be for us as well. Not only has God forgiven you, but He has forgotten what He's forgiven you for. "Forgive and forget" is not just a trite saying, but a model given to us by the God of all creation Himself. Ask Him to fill you with His power to move forward in your forgiveness of others. Allow God to restore your heart today by cleansing it with His forgiveness and giving you the power to forgive.

Notes

CHAPTER FIVE

Temptation and Deliverance through the Spirit of God

After petitioning God for Daily Bread and seeking forgiveness for self and others as discussed in the last few chapters, this prayer now seeks God's protection and guidance. Jesus reminds us that in this life we need God to lead us and to deliver us from the evil one.

> *And do not bring us into temptation, but deliver us from evil.* — **Matthew 6:13**

Matthew 6:13 is an unusual verse because throughout scripture, we are told that God does not tempt man.

> *Let no man say when he is tempted 'I am tempted of God.'* — **James 1:13**

Why is Jesus praying that God would not bring us into temptation if God does not tempt? At first glance this seems to be a contradiction. However, as we explore the text, we gain more understanding of what Jesus is saying.

On the surface it would seem that Jesus is asking God not to tempt or entice us to sin. In the prayer, Jesus implies that God has such control over us and the tempter that He can deliver us from our testing and trials if we call upon him. The Greek word for "tempt" that Jesus uses actually means to test or try. We can surmise then that Jesus, in the prayer, is asking God, the Father, not to lead us into more trials. Within the context of the entire Bible, we understand that trials will always come. In Matthew 6:34 Jesus says, "Don't worry about tomorrow, for tomorrow will bring its own worries. Today's trouble is enough for today." There are plenty of tests and trials that we will face outside of the schemes and tricks of the enemy. It is the testing by God that is designed to make us stronger. Before steel beams can be used in the construction of a skyscraper, the beams must be tested in order to determine the beams' strength. Like the beam, we too are tested and the prayer is a request for God to not let us break under the weight of the test.

The prayer is not asking that we never go through tests but that God would not add to our burden. The spirit led Jesus to be tested in the wilderness and we are no less than Jesus. It is during our time of testing that we discover how strong we really are. The enemy wants our test to become a temptation that we give into, ultimately leading to our destruction.

The trick of Satan is to always get us to fall. Therefore, within this prayer is a request to be delivered from the schemes of the enemy that are not meant for our good. On one hand, we are grateful for the test and need the Lord to help us get through it because we want to be stronger. On the other hand we need God's divine deliverance so that we can escape the trap of the enemy.

The testing alone is not evil. As explained earlier, God uses testing to strengthen us. It is the enemy that desires these tests to destroy us. Jesus prays that we would be delivered from the evil one. Psalm 34:19 says, "Many are the afflictions of the righteous, but the Lord delivers us out of them all." In 1 Corinthians 10:13, we learn that God will not allow us to be tempted beyond what we can bear, and that He will provide us a way to endure the test. If we do not take the way of escape, we will be tempted above what we are able. We will fall and give into sin. To avoid this outcome, we have to pray daily and ask God to deliver us.

Jesus demonstrates that we are to pray to God asking Him to keep us from undue testing and to deliver us from the evil one. However we have a responsibility to stay away from evil.

The Bible repeatedly instructs us to stay away from those things that we know would tempt and possibly cause us to stumble and fall. If we know we are weak in a certain area, why would we put ourselves in a place where we could fall? For example, if you struggle with alcohol, you are going to have enough temptation driving down the street, seeing all the bars and liquor stores without actually going in and sitting at the bar where you will be tempted. This is not God's doing. You are being drawn away by your own desires.

Once I was walking down the street I saw a little girl and her mother walking down the street. In the middle of the sidewalk was a large puddle. The little girl's mother told her to stay away from the puddle. What do you think she did? She tried to walk as close as she could without stepping in it but lost her balance and fell into the puddle. Why did she try to walk so close to the puddle? For the same reason we often try to get as close as we can to those things God tells us to stay away from. It is part of our sin nature. We try to get as close as we can to sin without falling. Yet too often we fall and then run to God asking Him to forgive and deliver us. When we are asking God to help us avoid temptation, we have to be sensitive to God's voice and obey His every command.

I was recently teaching at a teen seminar and asked the teens, "When you pray for God to direct you, what are some of the ways God will answer your prayer?" One young lady responded, "God always sends someone to me to tell me what I should and should not do." She went on to explain that every time she thought about doing wrong or being disobedient, someone, often a stranger, would come up to her and tell her not to. Likewise, we cannot expect God to do all the work to deliver us. God says, "Take part in this deliverance."

Do any of these statements sound familiar?

- "God, I want to walk closer with you" (As you're walking away).

- "God, lead me and guide me" (As you make your own decisions).

We cannot have the posture that we are following God when we are living outside of His will. Proverbs 14:12 says, "There is a way that seems right to a man, but in the end its road is death." This entire prayer points us to God, who is ultimately our source, our provider and our Lord. The key to living the Lord's Prayer is recognizing our relationship with the Father and totally submitting our lives to Him. Being free from those situations that could cause us to fall becomes much easier when we are walking in obedience to God's word and following His direction. God has a much better path that He wants us to follow.

Benediction

For Yours is the kingdom and the power and the glory forever — Matt 6:13

Jesus closes this prayer by bringing the attention back to God and His sovereign place in our relationship. This prayer opened with Jesus taking us to the Father and closes by reinforcing that He is our God and in total control. His reference to kingdom reminds us that everyplace we live, move and have our being belongs to Him. With each step we take throughout life, the kingdom moves with us.

Many of us were told that once we got saved, all we had to do was go to church, sing a few songs, give our offering and life would be easy. Many Christians think God exists to satisfy our every whim. However, we know this is not true, and our commitment to being a part of that kingdom comes with our allegiance to the King of Kings. Submission to God and following Him are nonnegotiable for anyone desiring to live the Lord's Prayer.

Throughout history people have followed leaders because they knew in following they would be led to a better life. Moses was the deliverer of the children of Israel, but they had to follow him to reach their deliverance. Harriet Tubman was also called "Moses." She was the deliverer of thousands of African slaves in this country, but they had to follow her and take part in their deliverance through the Underground Railroad. In both cases, the journeys were difficult, but the Promised Land on the other side far outweighed the struggles of the journey.

We need to rise to the challenge to live the Lord's Prayer. Life is already full of struggles and when we get saved, life becomes more difficult because the enemy focuses his attacks on us. Following God is not for the faint of heart. It takes faith and trust. We need His power; the power that rose Jesus from the dead to live the life he requires. This is the power Jesus references in this benediction. As believers we are able to access this power through our relationship with the Lord. We need to be yielded to the spirit of Christ and filled with His power. That is the only way we are going to be victorious. We can go to church every day, but if the

Spirit of God is not moving in your life, it will not make a difference.

> *Therefore, there is now no condemnation for those who are in Christ Jesus. For the law of the Spirit of life in Christ Jesus has set you free from the law of sin and of death. For what the Law could not do, weak as it was through the flesh, God did: sending His own Son in the likeness of sinful flesh and as an offering for sin, He condemned sin in the flesh, so that the requirement of the Law might be fulfilled in us, who do not walk according to the flesh but according to the Spirit.* — **Romans 8:1-5**

When we walk according to the spirit, we are not yielding to our flesh, thus, our flesh is not controlling us. That is how God wants us to live. This is how God is glorified through our lives. To glorify God means to shine a light of Him. Our lives need to be lived in such a way that everyone we encounter is pointed to Him and He will then have the glory forever.

I am glad Jesus ends this prayer in this way. After I have asked God to meet my needs, and to bless others, and to forgive me, then He fills me and guides me so that I can live a life that brings Him glory.

The bottom line is this: God is in control of our every breath and we must submit to Him. This prayer serves as the blueprint for our connection with God. Following the pattern of this prayer will not only allow God to move in our lives but will connect us with His presence. When we are connected and filled with God's Spirit, He will move and guide us into His perfect will.

Chapter Five Questions

Question: Have you ever felt tested by God? What was your response to Him? How did it make you feel, and did you take those feelings to Him in prayer?

_____

_____

_____

_____

_____

_____

_____

_____

_____

_____

_____

_____

_____

_____

_____

_____

Question: Reflect on your life. What have been your greatest temptations? How have you responded to them over the years? Are they still present in your life? Has your response changed? Does your response include prayer?

_____

_____

_____

_____

_____

_____

_____

_____

_____

_____

_____

_____

_____

_____

Question: How are you walking daily according to the Spirit? Are you aligned with Him, even when you feel tested or tempted?

_____

_____

_____

_____

_____

_____

_____

_____

_____

_____

_____

_____

_____

_____

_____

_____

Question: What does a life that brings Him glory look like to you? How does your life compare?

_____

_____

_____

_____

_____

_____

_____

_____

_____

_____

_____

_____

_____

_____

_____

_____

Action: Jesus gave us the blueprints to the prayer that we should pray. He has given us everything we need to know that He is in control, and He wants to bring good from our lives. But we also have a role to play. Make the choice today to seek Him actively in the decisions of your life.

Decide to pray to Him not only out of need and desire, but also out of gratitude and praise. Thank Him daily for the many blessings He has given you and the troubles He has saved you from. He longs to grow us into a daily dependence on Him, which fosters a close, intimate relationship in which we can hear His voice. As we grow closer to Him, His voice becomes clearer and we become more certain it is Him. Just as He knows our voice, we become able to recognize His.

Purpose today to follow hard after Jesus, digging daily into His Word and nourishing your soul the way He has intended. Protect your heart and mind from the enemy's plan to distract you, and stay focused on God's divine will for your life. Pray for all things, and have faith that He hears your heart and is faithful to answer. It is time to make the decision to not only pray as He did, but also to walk as He did. From this day forward, walk in the Spirit and be blessed.

Notes

_____
_____
_____
_____
_____
_____
_____
_____
_____
_____
_____
_____
_____
_____
_____
_____
_____
_____
_____
_____
_____
_____
_____
_____

About The Author

Pastor Michael Heath is the Sr. Pastor and founder of Living Waters Ministries located right outside of Philadelphia, Pa

With over 25 years of ministry experience, Pastor Heath is a much sought after preacher and revivalist. He has been a guest lecturer at Biblical Seminary and at various conferences throughout the country with the goal of equipping men and women with tools needed that will impact the lives of those both inside and outside of the church.

Pastor Heath attended Philadelphia College of the Bible and holds a Master of Divinity degree from Biblical Theological Seminary where he is currently pursuing a Doctor of Minister degree.

Encourage the Author by Reviewing This Book

If you've found this book helpful or challenging, the author would love your honest feedback. Please consider stopping by Amazon.com and writing a review.

To submit a review, simply go to *Living the Lord's Prayer's* Amazon.com page, click "Write a customer review" in the Customer Reviews section, and click submit.

Made in the USA
Middletown, DE
05 February 2016